The Night Before Mardi Gras

Written and Illustrated by Gail Perkins Nettles

Copyright © 2008 by Gail Perkins Nettles
All rights reserved.

ISBN-13: 978-1517069421

ISBN-10: 1517069424

About the Author

Gail Perkins Nettles has spent a lifetime educating young children. Now she enjoys writing and illustrating books to help inspire a love for reading. Gail has two children, five beautiful grandchildren, and lives in Baton Rouge, Louisiana with her husband and their Yorkie, Shadeaux. Mardi Gras is a fun time for her for she is a member of the Krewe of Romany and attends many Mardi Gras parades and parties every year.

Dedication

This book is dedicated to my five precious grandchildren,

Katherine, Grant, Alexandra, Gage, & Caroline.

I have the most fun when I watch a parade through their eyes.

Mimi loves each and every one of you!

Happy Mardi Gras!

It was the night before Mardi Gras
and all through the South,
not one child was stirring.
They were all sacked out!

They had to be good
so they went straight to bed
to get plenty of rest
for the big day ahead.

They snuggled and snored
and dreamed the night away
of floats and beads
and an exciting Mardi Gras Day!

Up they arose
with a great big yawn
and threw on their costumes,
although it was barely dawn.

They jumped in the car.
They could hardly wait
to see the parade,
and they couldn't be late!

When out on the street,
we saw such a scene.
The floats were Mardi Gras colors—
purple, gold and green.

As they rolled by,
the children would shout,
"Throw me something, Mister!"
while jumping all about.

Beads and doubloons
were flying through the air.
The children were snatching them
without any care.

Parade-goers wore masks
with feathers and such.
Their costumes were fancy
with a colorful touch.

Everyone was celebrating and dancing to the beat of the Mardi Gras music all out in the street.

When the parade was over
and the King and Queen were done,
everyone was happy
and had lots of fun!

So many good memories
of a great Mardi Gras Day
left the children sad
because they couldn't stay.

They waved goodbye
and shed a tear,
but they'll be back
again next year.

So they ate boiled crawfish,
king cake and beignets, too.
Then it was time
to bid all adieu!

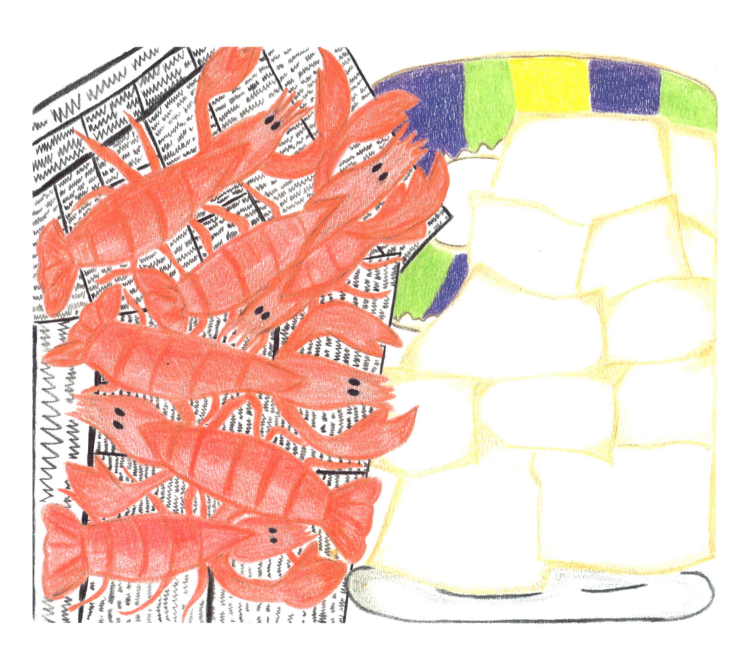

Then they heard them cheer
as they drove out of sight,
"Happy Mardi Gras to all
and to all a good night!"

But, wait a minute!

That was only the night BEFORE Mardi Gras!
Can you believe it was only a dream?
Now the clock ticks time to go,
and have the best Mardi Gras you've ever seen.

Glossary

Mardi Gras Beads: A thin string of beads made from plastic in different colors that krewe members on the float like to throw to parade-goers.

Beignets: A beignet is a French doughnut that is deep fried and sprinkled with powdered sugar.

Costumes: It is a tradition to wear crazy fun clothes to Mardi Gras.

Crawfish: A crawfish is a freshwater crustacean that resembles a small lobster. They can be eaten boiled, fried, stewed, and many other ways.

Doubloons: A doubloon is a medallion or coin that usually has the name of a Krewe or King on it. Krewe members throw them to special parade-goers.

Float: A float is a large vehicle that has been elaborately decorated for a parade.

King Cake: A King cake is a ring of dough shaped into an oval and decorated with colored sugars. A plastic baby is inserted after the cake is baked and the person getting the slice with the baby is asked to buy the next king cake.

Mardi Gras: Mardi Gras is music, parades, picnics, floats, balls, excitement, and one big holiday.

Mardi Gras Colors: Rex, the King of Carnival, selected the colors, so purple, green and gold are the official Mardi Gras colors. Purple stands for justice, green for faith, and gold for power.

Mardi Gras Parade: Is a procession of people celebrating Mardi Gras, including decorated vehicles or floats, marching bands, and even people on horseback.

Mardi Gras Music: Music played at Mardi Gras is usually very lively, loud jazz.

Mardi Gras Mask: It is traditional to wear a mask at Mardi Gras. Some wear them to catch the attention from the float riders in order to get more throws.

More Fun with Mardi Gras
for
Parents and Teachers!

☆To encourage language, read other books about Mardi Gras.

☆To encourage creativity, let the children glue different colored Mardi Gras beads on stiff paper to create a work of art. Make a mask and let the children decorate it with feathers, sequins, colored paper, etc. Let them decorate a bike or wagon to resemble a float.

☆To practice math concepts, help the children count the beads or doubloons. See how many different colors were collected. See what color has the greatest numbers of beads, what color has the least number of beads, etc. Graph the results. Add or subtract the beads. Line the beads up from the smallest to the largest.

☆To encourage music appreciation, play Mardi Gras or Jazz music and allow the children to move creatively to the music. This would be a good time to introduce different genres of music. Let them pretend they are in a parade and march.

☆Have the children practice saying this tongue twister—the faster they try to say it, the more fun they'll have: Mardi Gras mainly makes merry music.

☆To encourage science skills, make king cakes by using canned biscuits. See next page for directions.

King Cakes for Kids

Ingredients:

Canned biscuits

Cinnamon and granulated sugar mixture

Colored granulated sugar (purple, yellow, green)

Powdered sugar

Water

Each child gets two uncooked biscuits and they roll them out in the shape of ropes. Roll the "ropes" in the cinnamon and sugar mixture. Pinch the tops of the ropes together, twist them around each other and pinch the ends to make a circle. Bake according to the directions on the can.

Make icing with powdered sugar and hot water. Mix until it is thick enough to drizzle on the cake. Dye the granulated sugar by putting it and a few drops of food coloring in a ziplock bag. Mix until the color is even. Add more food coloring until the sugar is the desired color. Do this for all three colors.

Drizzle the icing on the cakes and sprinkle the colored sugar on top. Eat and enjoy!

CPSIA information can be obtained
at www.ICGtesting.com
Printed in the USA
LVHW072338080121
676099LV00002B/28